BRUCE POON TIP

FOUNDER OF G ADVENTURES

An imprint of Harper Collins Publishers Ltd.

This book is dedicated to those who want to explore this life.

If you are willing to take yourself away from what's familiar and journey into the unknown...

If you believe there is something more out there...

If you are determined to find your place in the universe...

If you understand that living is the rarest thing in the world, because most of us just exist...

this Book is for you

THIS is my JOURNEY

X _____
          NAME

THUMBPRINT

HOW to USE this BOOK

take IT WITH YOU
ROUGH it UP
GIVE it AWAY
RECORD everything
invite OTHERs
but MOST
IMPORTANTLY...

GET this
BOOK
DIRTY

START WITH THIS PAGE

THE WORLD IS A VAST, EVER-CHANGING, AWE-INSPIRING PLACE.

It is the only home any of us have ever known — yet only a few venture to see it.

As the founder of a travel company, I've seen first-hand how society creates tourists, spectators who prefer an arms-length, armchair view of the world. But we were born to be explorers, with the curiosity to discover. And getting to know how other people live, understanding cultures that are so different than our own, is the fastest path to peace.

Every saint, sinner, hero and villain is warmed by the same sun. Each of us fights for meaning beneath the same moon. All of us must leave our own borders to find freedom, to climb our own mountains of growth, to cross our own bridges for connection. We all have to discover our part in something bigger.

Travel can be that vehicle, but you don't have to go far from home to experience this big, bad, beautiful, perfect planet. From where you are standing right now, you have the choice to go backward, stand still or move forward. There is no wrong answer, but there is significance in everything you do. The winding path, the tiny choices, the big mistakes, the unexpected encounters you experience will shape your ability to become a better version of yourself.

This book is a map, a diversion, a path to meaningful connections. It can mark moments in time that you will one day pass on to your children. It is a record of all the big small things you do.

So get on your way.

THE JOURNEY WILL CHANGE YOU.

PEACE,
Bruce

FREEDOM GROW

BE A PART OF SOMETH

i ONCE SPENT A long NIGHT in A BURMESE border PRISON

I realized then how easy it is to forget how free we are.

People don't put themselves out there because they think they can't — too many rules, responsibilities, and expectations.

But if you are carrying this book around,

make No mistake

I AM free to Do WHAT i WANt

make your list

_____   _____

_____   _____

_____   _____

_____   _____

_____   _____

_____   _____

_____   _____

_____   _____

_____   _____

_____   _____

_____   _____

_____   _____

WHAT could Stop You?

cross it out

WHEN WE GET TOO
Comfortable WE SETTLE
for THE FAMILIAR

TRUTH is,
IF you want THE COMFORTS OF
HOME, you SHOULD
STAY HOME
BUT if you WANT to BE
FREE...

List -THE- COMFORTS you're willing to LEAVE BEHIND

Fear does not exist.
It is a figment created from
our ignorance of the unknown.
It blocks the fastest path to peace,
which is getting to know
our brothers and sisters
who share this planet.

PUSH PAST it

WARRIOR TRIBES of the AMAZON BELIEVE WE have A PREDETERMINED number of HEARTBEATS

those WHO Live IN FEAR use THEM UP Faster

I WILL NO LONGER
WASTE HEARTBEATS ON...

D

it's time to go
RIGHT NOW
AWAY from here
No Dilly
No DALLY
OUT there
Where EVERYTHING
is HAPPENING

NOTHING GETS YOU MOVING
LIKE A MUSICAL COMPANION
WRITE YOUR PLAYLIST

_____

_____

_____

_____

_____

_____

_____

_____

_____

_____

Places i WANT to Go

in your neighborhood, on the other side
of town, over the border, across the ocean,
off the beaten track, beyond reason

_____   _____

_____   _____

_____   _____

_____   _____

_____   _____

_____   _____

_____   _____

_____   _____

_____   _____

HERE'S the FIRST place i WENT on the List

return with a Souvenir for this page

log the way you traveled

HOW	WHERE	WHEN

PROOF of TRANSIT

TICKET STUBS, transfers, BOARDING PASSES and *Camel Hoofprints* GO HERE

My girlfriend and I wanted the most budget-friendly option to get us from Sapa, in the northern mountains of Vietnam, to Dien Bien Phu – a halfway point on our longer journey into Laos. We knew it wouldn't be comfortable, but our best bet was to hop into a twelve-seater minibus for $11 USD each.

We crammed ourselves in, to the point where any space for oxygen was squeezed out by someone's bottom or luggage. I threw out everything I knew about road safety, and accepted that my fate was in the hands of a man who may have decided to be a bus driver earlier that day because he needed the work. Defensive driving barely describes the aggressive skill our driver needed to get us to our destination. We navigated turn after turn, dodging pockets of craters that dotted the road. At one point, it started to pour down rain. Our minibus didn't have windshield wipers, but somehow the driver maintained our speed through such poor visibility.

I spent eleven uncomfortable hours holding onto my seat and reflecting on the virtue of patience. Our bus stopped to pick up and let off hitchhikers or packages frequently. I repented for the times I threatened to file a complaint with city council about a subway delay back home.

An old Korean man sat behind me cross-legged through the entire journey. He never uttered a single word to anyone and mostly kept his eyes closed. I figured he had found a Buddha-like calm to get him through. I tried to do the same and thought of things that made me happy.

Eventually, two hitchhikers joined our entourage. They brought along two cages with live birds in each one. At a brief stop on our travels, one of the hitchhikers accidently knocked a cage over, letting a bird loose into the trees above us. No matter how hard he tried, he couldn't get the bird back.

Laughter is a universal language, and everyone onboard united for that moment to revel in the folly of life. Sometimes, you just have to laugh it off. It's part of the adventure.

you will be free when you are yourself

Do you know who you are?
Take this Quiz

1. YOU ARE A VIRTUE. YOU ARE:

   ☐ COMPASSION ☐ HONESTY ☐ OTHER _____

   ☐ PERSEVERANCE ☐ LOYALTY

2. YOU ARE PART OF THE EARTH. YOU ARE:

   ☐ MOUNTAIN ☐ FOREST ☐ OTHER _____

   ☐ LAKE ☐ PRAIRIE

3. YOU ARE ANCIENT. YOU ARE:

   ☐ PYRAMIDS ☐ WATERFALL ☐ OTHER _____

   ☐ MYTH ☐ SCRIPTURE

4. YOU ARE AN ANIMAL. YOU ARE:

   ☐ ELEPHANT ☐ LION ☐ OTHER _____

   ☐ EAGLE ☐ DOLPHIN

5. YOU ARE WEATHER. YOU ARE:

   ☐ SUNSHINE ☐ SNOW ☐ OTHER _____

   ☐ RAIN ☐ TORNADO

TEAR THIS PAGE OUT WHEN BOTH QUIZZES ARE DONE

Do THEY KNOW who You ARE?
Give THIS Quiz

① THE KEEPER OF THIS BOOK IS A VIRTUE. THEY ARE:

☐ Compassion ☐ Honesty ☐ OTHER _____

☐ Perseverance ☐ Loyalty

② THE KEEPER OF THIS BOOK IS A PART OF THE EARTH. THEY ARE:

☐ Mountain ☐ Forest ☐ OTHER _____

☐ Lake ☐ Prairie

③ THE KEEPER OF THIS BOOK IS ANCIENT. THEY ARE:

☐ Pyramids ☐ Waterfall ☐ OTHER _____

☐ Myth ☐ Scripture

④ THE KEEPER OF THIS BOOK IS AN ANIMAL. THEY ARE:

☐ Elephant ☐ Lion ☐ OTHER _____

☐ Eagle ☐ Dolphin

⑤ THE KEEPER OF THIS BOOK IS WEATHER. THEY ARE:

☐ Sunshine ☐ Snow ☐ OTHER _____

☐ Rain ☐ Tornado

There are moments that put
 a knot in the pit of your stomach —
 a twinge of doubt accompanied
  by the urge to leap.

FREEDOM is calling

The secret to happiness is freedom,
and the secret to freedom is courage.
In Vanuatu, an island in the South Pacific,
they dive off wooden towers that rise 90 feet above
the earth with nothing but two vines tied to their ankles.
Their heads nearly touch the ground.

SOMETHING BOLD

What DID you Do?

it WILL Not BE
WHAT you EXPEC

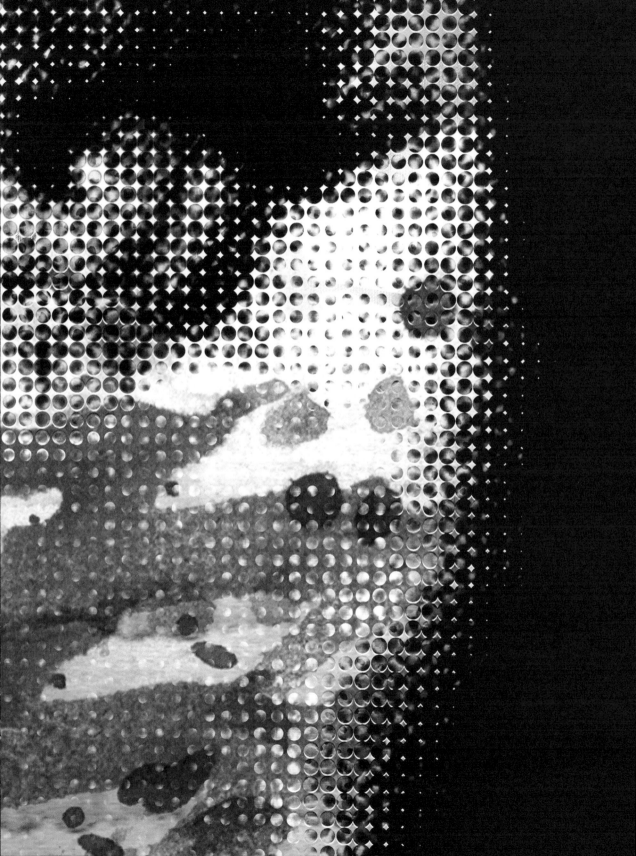

STUNNING staggering SURPRISING Moments

CAPTURE them HERE

I was Phoenix bound from Toronto
and after multiple missed flights due
to weather, being in cities I was never
meant to be in, after many tears, I ended
up in Las Vegas and it was soooooo cold
in the airport.

I finally fell asleep on a bench, shivering
so hard that my jaw hurt. I had a dream
that a middle aged Indian man put a
blanket on me. We didn't exchange
words, but he seemed caring.

I woke up to see that I had a blanket on
me. I guess I wasn't dreaming after all.

NEVER forget
where you came from

Discover
NATURE

Let WISDOM in

EVOLVE with EXPERIENCE

GET BACK UP.

MAKE Mistakes

Step Up

MEASURE yourself

MEASURE

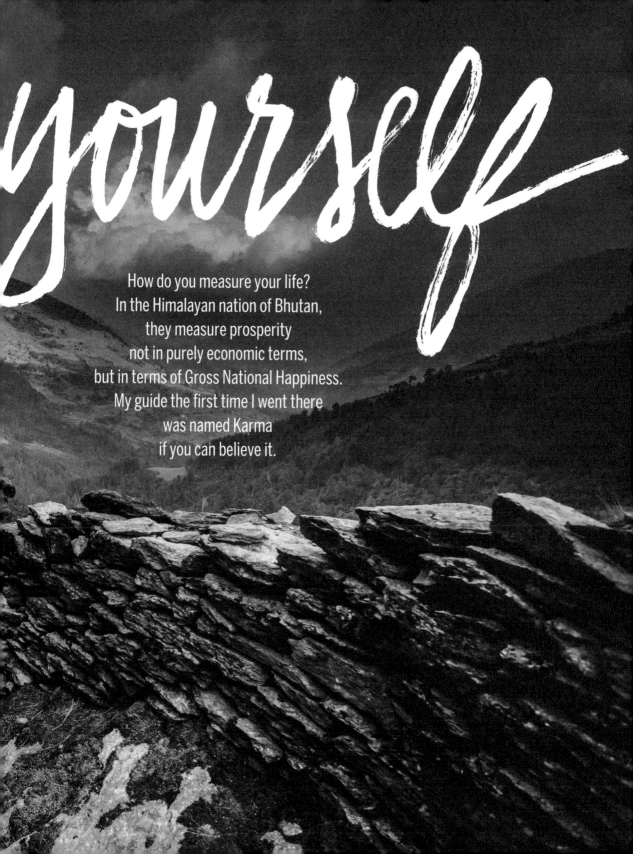

yourself

How do you measure your life?
In the Himalayan nation of Bhutan,
they measure prosperity
not in purely economic terms,
but in terms of Gross National Happiness.
My guide the first time I went there
was named Karma
if you can believe it.

MEASURE your GROS

MAKE a PIE chart of how you SPEND YOUR TIME

PERSONAL Happiness

MAKE A **PIE CHART** OF What MAKES You HAPPY

Often in travel, and in life, we cannot control our situations. One time, on the way from Houy Xai to Pakbeng, our bus overheated and broke down in a remote mountain village. Everyone in the village came out to greet us.

It was a hot day and they didn't hesitate to share their drinking water – to help us cool down the overheated bus. I didn't see any wells on that mountain, so I can't even imagine how long it must have taken to collect that water. And then they offered it to us –strangers. Everyone seemed truly shocked that these poor people not only helped us without asking for anything in return, but were happy to do so.

Travelers often express amazement at the kindness of poor people in remote places. I can see them wondering how they would react if a similar situation happened back home.

When we appreciate the actions of others, we become more aware of our own behaviour. It makes us better people.

Sokhorn

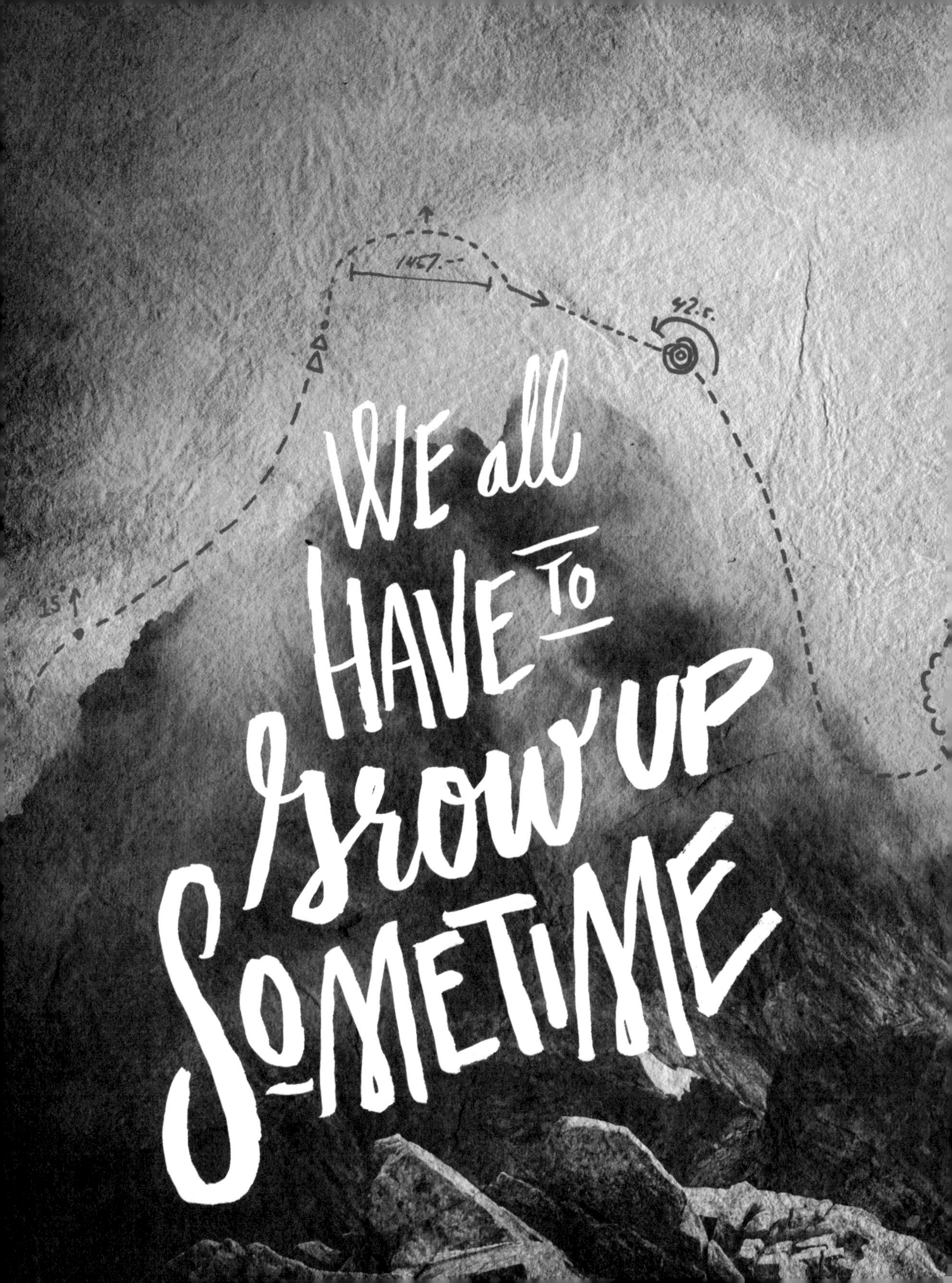
We all
Have to
grow up
Sometime

to BECOME MEN

Maasai boys are given spears, sent into the Savannah
and told not to return until they have killed a lion.

to BECOME A WOMAN

a Navajo girl lies down as her mother's hands hover over her body,
molding her into the woman she is becoming.
When she rises, she can mold others into the tribe.

this WAS MY RITE
of passage

this _is_ ADVICE for my
younger self

this was THE MOMENT
i knew i'd grown up

this is ADVICE for my
FUTURE SELF

Discover Nature

Sometimes, you have to leave the noise behind to hear what the universe is telling you

DISCOVERED in NATURE

SMEAR SOME MUD, draw a picture, MAKE A RUBBING, press a LEAF, WRITE WHAT you REALIZED

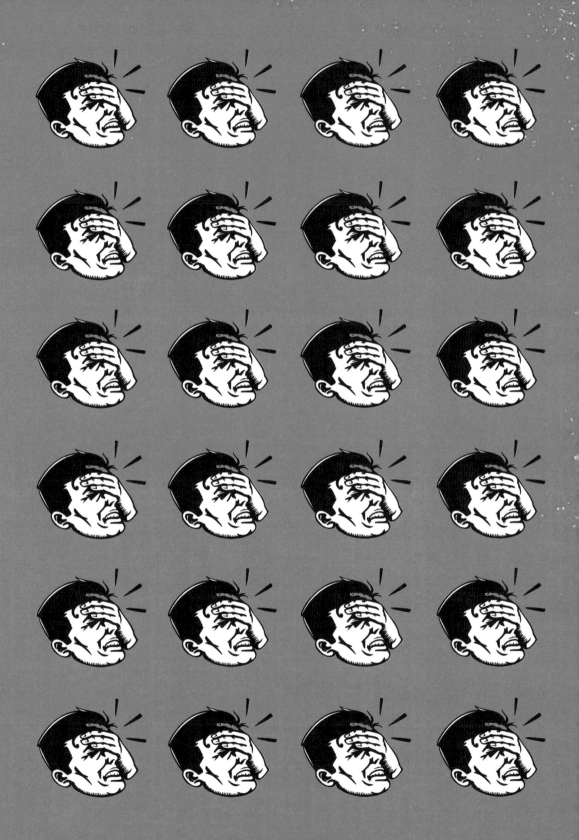

MAKE ~~mistakes~~ mistakes

You know who never makes mistakes? People who never do anything.

In Japan, giant torches are paraded around the base of Nachi Falls to burn away the wrongs of the past.

HERE'S <u>A</u> mistake i made

TEAR it OUT & let it GO

- -

HERE'S WHAT i Would Do Differently

It's NEVER too LATE

WABI
SABI

it's JAPANESE
for the flawed,
fleeting, incomplete beauty of EVERYTHING

it DOESN'T MATTER
how MANY times
you fall

Get BACK
up

After three surgeries and four rounds of chemotherapy, I was depressed, exhausted and overwhelmed. A close friend told me she was worried that cancer had turned me into a negative and bitter person. Thankfully an article on New Year's resolutions helped me find a way out. It suggested I choose three words to describe how I wanted to feel in the coming year – I chose healthy, loved, and inspired.

I knew volunteering in Africa would inspire me, and with the support of friends and family, I managed to raise $8,000 to participate in a six-week volunteer program in the Townships of Cape Town. There, I crashed into love with a group of mischievous one-to-three year olds, met women my age who had lost entire families to AIDS, and saw more joy on the faces of people who struggled to provide their families with the basic necessities of life than I had felt while earning a six figure salary.

The people I met had no preconceived notion of who I 'should' be. They didn't know the pre-cancer Terri, and I had the gift of being exactly who I was in that moment. I was me. And the opportunity to take care of toddlers let me forget for a while just how recently I had been the one that needed to be taken care of. Africa put my recent struggle in perspective. I felt loved and healed in a way I wouldn't have thought possible.

Since then, I've been inspired to help other people who have experienced cancer find a way to start fresh. The Fresh Chapter Alliance Foundation uses volunteering and meaningful travel to help people heal the emotional scars of cancer while fulfilling their dreams. So far, we've taken three groups to India where they have volunteered and stood marveling in awe at the beauty of the Taj Mahal.

On the journey, they come to see that even when nothing turns out the way you imagined, life can be extraordinary.

Terri

What BROUGHT you DOWN	How you Got up

EVOLVE with EXPERIENCE

WE ARE ALL WORKS IN PROGRESS

Above the Arctic Circle,
where there are few
natural landmarks,
the Inuit erect Inuksuit
to help you find your way.

MAKE

your LANDMARK

Fill pieces with the experiences that shaped you

the WORLD is A GREAT teacher

He told me to inhale deeply through my nose, taking in all the beauty in the world. "Flowers, trees, birds, happiness. Breathe them in. You will be stronger. Then exhale slowly, all the bad things. Sadness. Watch me." I was sitting cross-legged on a soft tatami mat with my back against a wooden post.

I looked at him: head shaved and dressed in blue cotton, he inhaled deeply as he moved his hands rhythmically through the air around his body, eyes shut behind aviator lenses. He opened his mouth slightly and exhaled the longest, steadiest, calmest breath.

Minutes later his eyes opened, "Your breath can go across the world and come back to you. In Buddhism, the Universe is very big but your heart is just as big. The world, your heart, the same."

Did he know? The chaotic emotions within me were overwhelming. I was a few weeks into my first trip to Japan and I planned to stay for a year. It was beautiful and strange, but this new environment had me so anxious and disoriented I had even lost my appetite – and I'd come here to eat. Self-doubt was winning. Would I make it?

I closed my eyes and inhaled so deeply that my breath seemed to start all the way back home. My mind's eye watched it travel over lakes, prairies, and mountains, getting stronger as it moved west across the Pacific towards me. I let it fill my lungs and became still.

And then I exhaled, long and slow. My unease began to dissipate, replaced by a growing courage.

I opened my eyes. I looked at the man before me, a monk. This was his world and I was in it now and it would be good. He led me out of the temple and into the kitchen where his wife had breakfast on the table and the family's miniature dachshund waited, tail wagging. I sat down to eat, hungry at last.

WORDS of Wisdom

invite others to share some

PEOPLE I ADMIRE

& what they TAUGHT ME

His Holiness the DALAI Lama

FOR HIS Compassion

Steve JOBS FOR INNOVATION

ROALD AMUNDSEN

the FIRST EXPLORER to REACH the South Pole in 1911
for BEING A true ADVENTURER. INSPIRED BY HIM,
i MADE MY OWN Journey TO ANTARCTICA ON THE
100 year ANNIVERSARY of HIS DISCOVERY.

PEOPLE you ADMIRE

what HAVE they TAUGHT you?

A BOOK will CHANGE you

GIVE SOMEONE a book THAT MARKED you

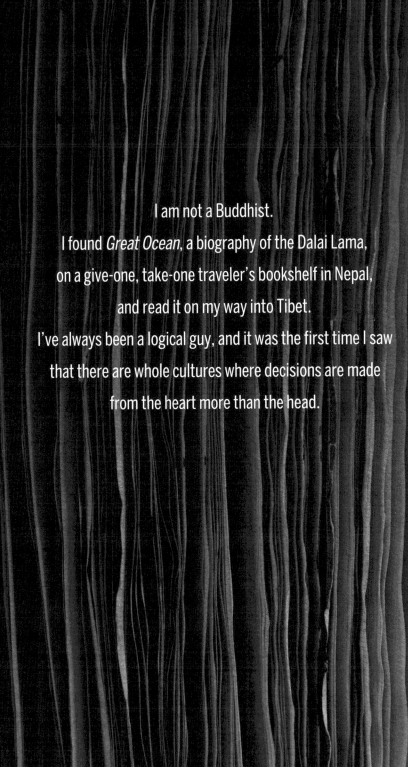

I am not a Buddhist.

I found *Great Ocean*, a biography of the Dalai Lama,

on a give-one, take-one traveler's bookshelf in Nepal,

and read it on my way into Tibet.

I've always been a logical guy, and it was the first time I saw

that there are whole cultures where decisions are made

from the heart more than the head.

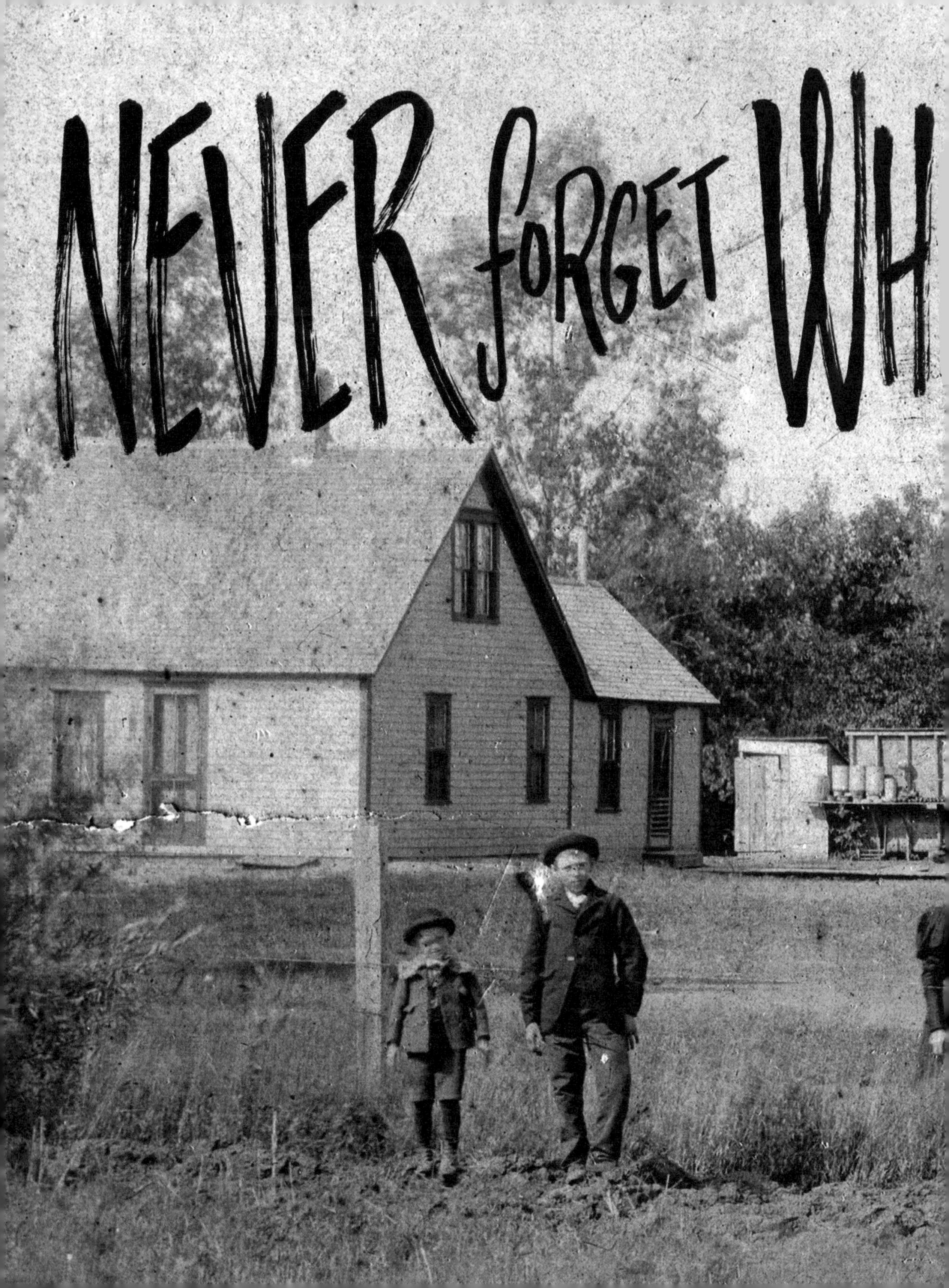
NEVER forget WH

you CAME from

RECALL your CHILDHOOD HOME

Bring back a memory.

WHENEVER I HEAR this SONG   HERE'S WHERE it TAKES ME

_____   _____

_____   _____

                            _____

                            _____

_____   _____

                            _____

_____   _____

                            _____

                            _____

_____   _____

                            _____

_____   _____

                            _____

When I met Tom, it was like greeting my Nonno – grandfather in Italian.

We said hello for the first time with a double-sided kiss on the cheek, and sat down on plastic chairs in the backyard. I was in Melbourne visiting family, and Tom was the Italian neighbor who tended a big, green garden out back.

Tom brought out his homemade wine and plunked it on the concrete in the middle of our chairs. He balanced a wooden cutting board on his knee and started slicing thin pieces of homemade pancetta. My heart warmed. It was like sitting with my Nonno and chatting over good food and wine, except I was on the other side of the world from my native Canada.

My dad was born in Italy, and while I was born in Canada, I've always identified more with my Italian roots.

We shared stories about our families over sips of vino tinto. Tom emigrated from Italy to Melbourne in his 20s, worked in construction, and started a family. My Nonno emigrated to Canada in the 1950s, where he worked on the railway and raised a family. Now, they were both in their 70s and 80s, handsome and fit, and still passionate and proud about their culture.

Every once in a while, Tom would retreat through his gate to offer something else: homemade salami, olives, cheese and more wine. Slowly, the sky turned into streaks of pink and blue. The more I said "don't worry" when asked if I wanted more food and wine, the more Tom insisted. He was just like my Nonno. He didn't want the moment to end. That evening as the sky turned black, we said goodbye with another double-sided kiss on the cheek.

My Nonno died unexpectedly while I was still in Australia. Meeting Tom was a moment to cherish my roots, when I couldn't be with my Nonno back home.

Kristen

SPAN GENERATIONS
feel THE Love
CREATE TOGETHER
HELLO FRIEND
ER

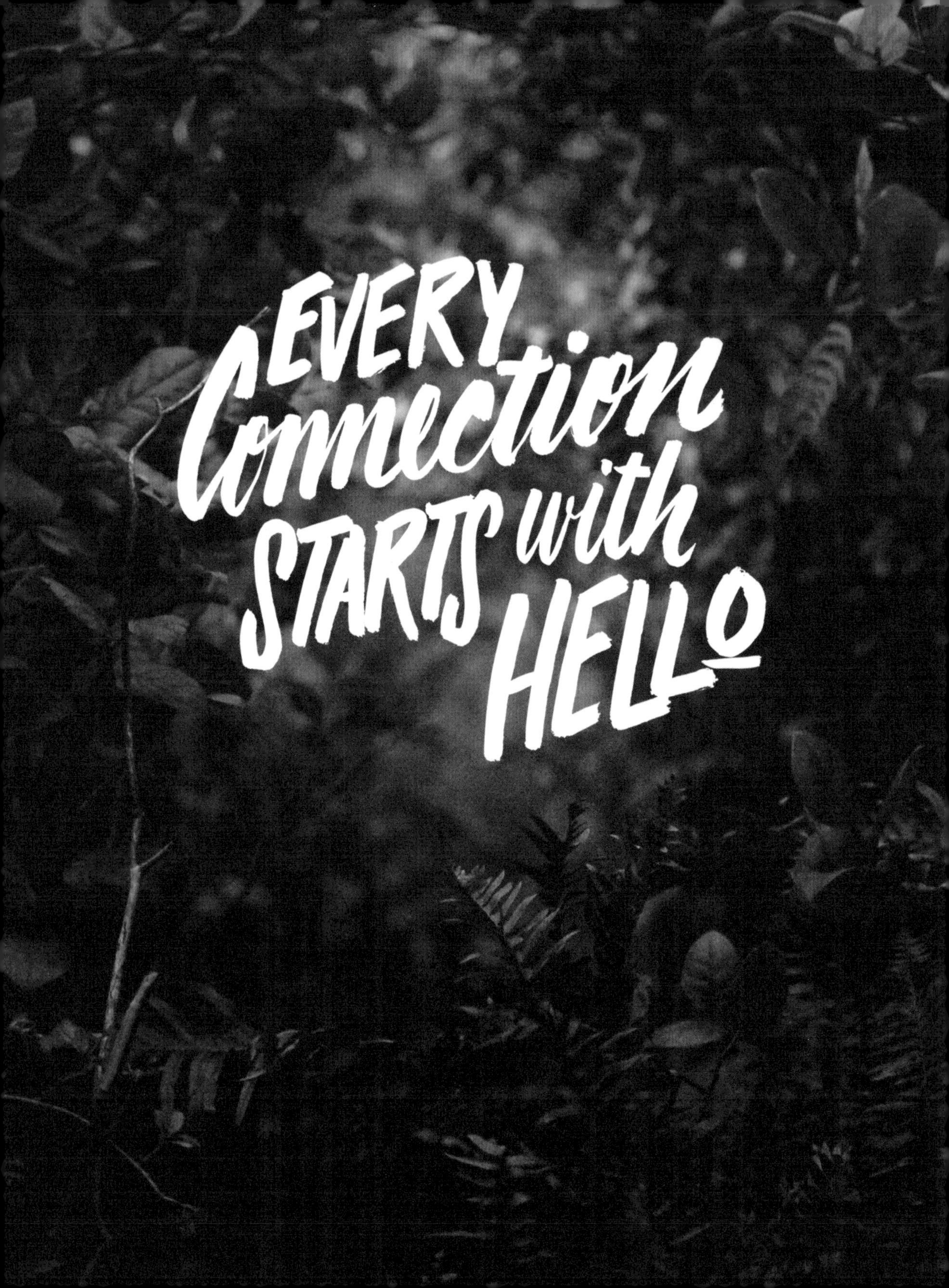
EVERY
Connection
STARTS with
HELLO

IN Belgium, they GIVE three KISSES, MOVING from CHEEK to CHEEK

in PARTS of FRANCE, THEY GIVE four

the Japanese BOW SLIGHTLY from the WAIST

in the MIDDLE EAST, they use THE SALAAM, SAYING "peace BE UPON you" and SWEEPING their RIGHT HANDS to their HEARTS

in ZIMBABWE, they CLAP

TIBETANS may STICK their TONGUES OUT

the MĀORI RUB NOSES

Latin AMERICANS hug ALOT

MALAYS reach OUT, SANDWICH each other's fingertips, & BRING their HANDS BACK to their CHESTS

in THAILAND, it's A SLIGHT BOW with PALMS PRESSED together. the HIGHER the HANDS, the GREATER the SHOW of RESPECT

I ONCE MET A WARRIOR WHO LIVED IN THE RAINFOREST.

Delfin lived according to principles handed down by his ancestors, surviving off the lushness of the Amazon jungle. He was a proud man who had little or no interest in the outside world.

Although we came from wildly different places and didn't speak the same language, we recognized something in one another. We shared the same values.

We managed with silent gestures when there wasn't an interpreter around. I told Delfin my dream: I wanted to start a travel company and bring people to his village to see how he lived day-to-day with his tribe and family. I could tell that he didn't quite understand, but he just trusted me. He took me down to the river, smeared mud on my face and covered me in herbs to cleanse me of evil spirits.

Over the next twenty-five years, Delfin and I grew up together—not seeing each other very often, but forming a bond of brotherhood. We hug sometimes when I return to his corner of the Amazon, but that's a Western thing and I think Delfin only does it for my sake. Then he covers me with mud and herbs because I've collected spirits during our time apart.

We're older, wiser, and greyer now, although Delfin doesn't know exactly how old he is using our calendar years. I have watched his kids grow up. They are raising their own young families, living in the rainforest, following their proud traditions. Many tribes have since abandoned the old ways, so it's lonelier out there.

Through an interpreter, Delfin always tells me, "Remember, Bruce, we are warmed by the same sun." I think of his words on hot summer days when I find myself walking through a concrete urban jungle, and imagine my friend feeling the sun's warmth in his own jungle far away.

Delfin taught me that life is measured not by how many people you know, but by the meaningful connections you make. There have never been two more unlikely friends, but we came together because our hearts were open all those years ago.

Chance encounters are karma's way of opening doors.
If you're ready and willing, you can bet that your life
will be changed by someone you haven't met yet.

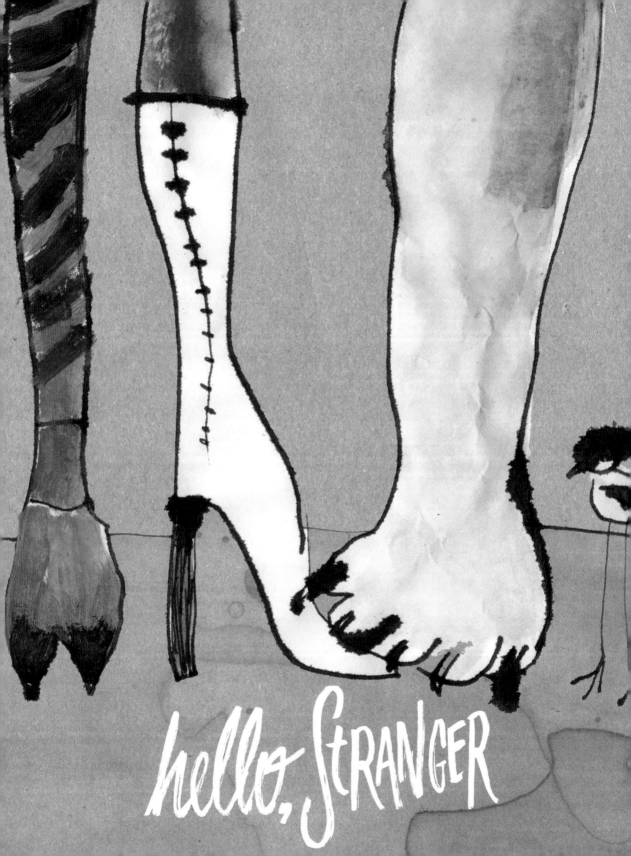

LET THEM Draw you

It all started with a $1.50 tip. On the trip of a lifetime, my wife and I were having dinner in the central market in Siem Reap, Cambodia. The bill came to $3.50, and we gave our waiter $5.00. When we told him to keep the change, he was overwhelmed by our generosity. Touched by his reaction, we returned the next night, and the same thing happened. He thanked us and said the money would help him pay for school.

On our way back to our hotel, my wife and I stopped in our tracks. We had seen so much poverty and human suffering here. We felt the need to do something … anything. Without saying a word, we made our way back to the restaurant.

The waiter's name was Rady. He was abandoned by his parents when he was five. At ten, while in a tree collecting coconuts to sell for food, he looked into the distance and saw hundreds of kids in school uniforms. He followed them, and begged and pleaded with the headmaster until he was allowed to attend.

Now Rady wanted to go further. We ended up paying for him to go to college. A few years later, we helped raise $1,400 for him to buy a tuk-tuk, so he could be fully independent. Soon enough, he had a small fleet.

Here's the best part. Eventually, Rady sold one of the tuk-tuks so he could build a school of his own. He wanted to provide free English classes to local children, so they could have the same opportunities he had.

Now our friend Rady has three schools in three different areas, teaching more than 750 children.

All that, from a $1.50 tip, a bit of kindness and faith from strangers, and the determination of one boy who wanted to make his world a little better.

Neil

Stories of UNFORGETTABLE people i MET

MAKE Someone's DAY
PASS A NOTE

you OKAY?

GREAT smile

i BELIEVE in you

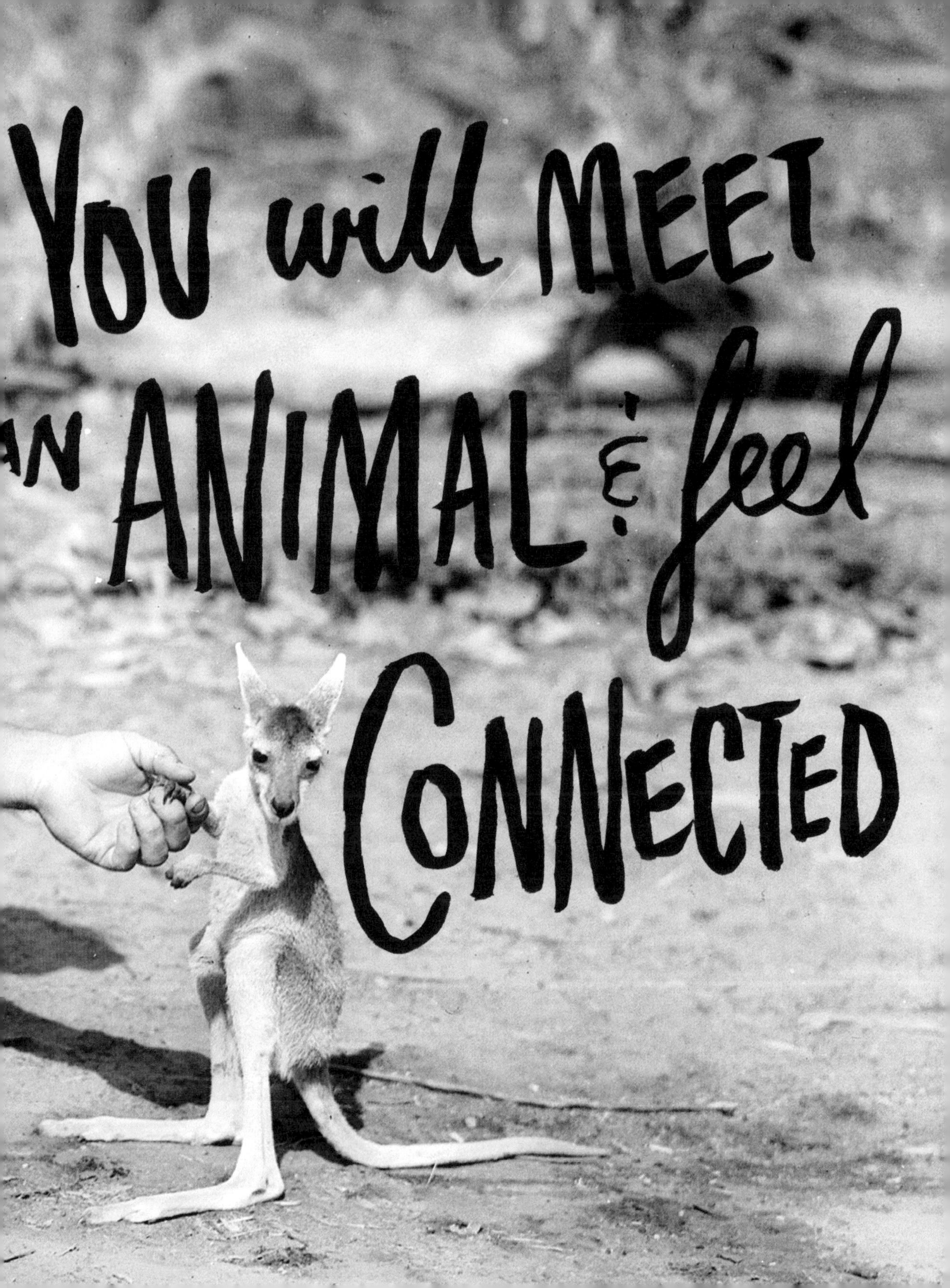
YOU will MEET
AN ANIMAL & feel
CONNECTED

ASK for an ANIMA

OOTPRINT

IT WAS IMPOSSIBLY HOT AS WE TREKKED THROUGH THE MOUNTAIN FOREST.

Our guide was dressed in army green, swinging his machete to clear the brush. The dense canopy overhead made a dark pressure cooker that held in the heat of the high noon sun.

Our excitement had long ago slipped into exhaustion. But then, suddenly, our guide's hand shot up, motioning for everyone to stop. He arched his back and sniffed the air. Then he smiled and tapped his finger towards a wall of green foliage that seemed like all the others we'd seen all day.

His blade bore down. Its swing covered a wide area, and the wall dropped like a curtain before our eyes.

There was a collective gasp. A few short feet in front of us, behind where the green wall had been, sat a family of twelve mountain gorillas. Everyone in our group was stunned and quickly bowed down low.

The gorillas turned their heads slightly to see what all the fuss was about. Unfazed, they didn't stop what they were doing on this lazy afternoon. I had read that mountain gorillas don't get scared when they see humans, because they recognize our shape as familiar.

It was impossible not to look, even though we were strictly instructed not to make eye contact immediately. With my head bowed, I glanced up and saw a female chewing on some shoots. She was staring directly at me. Our eyes locked.

I stood motionless. Breathless.

The connection was unlike any I'd felt before. I saw a soul in the deep light brown eyes of this creature who was looking back at me. Looking at me like I was familiar to her. Like I was family.

She walked up to me and playfully pulled on my backpack. And in that moment, my connection with nature was forever changed.

My FRIENDS

can fill these pages however they want

on long BITTER DAYS when the SUN barely RISES AND the STORMS RAGE on, SCANDINAVIANS know where to find WARMTH — with friends.

the DANES call it HYGGELIG

the NORWEGIANS call it KOSELIG

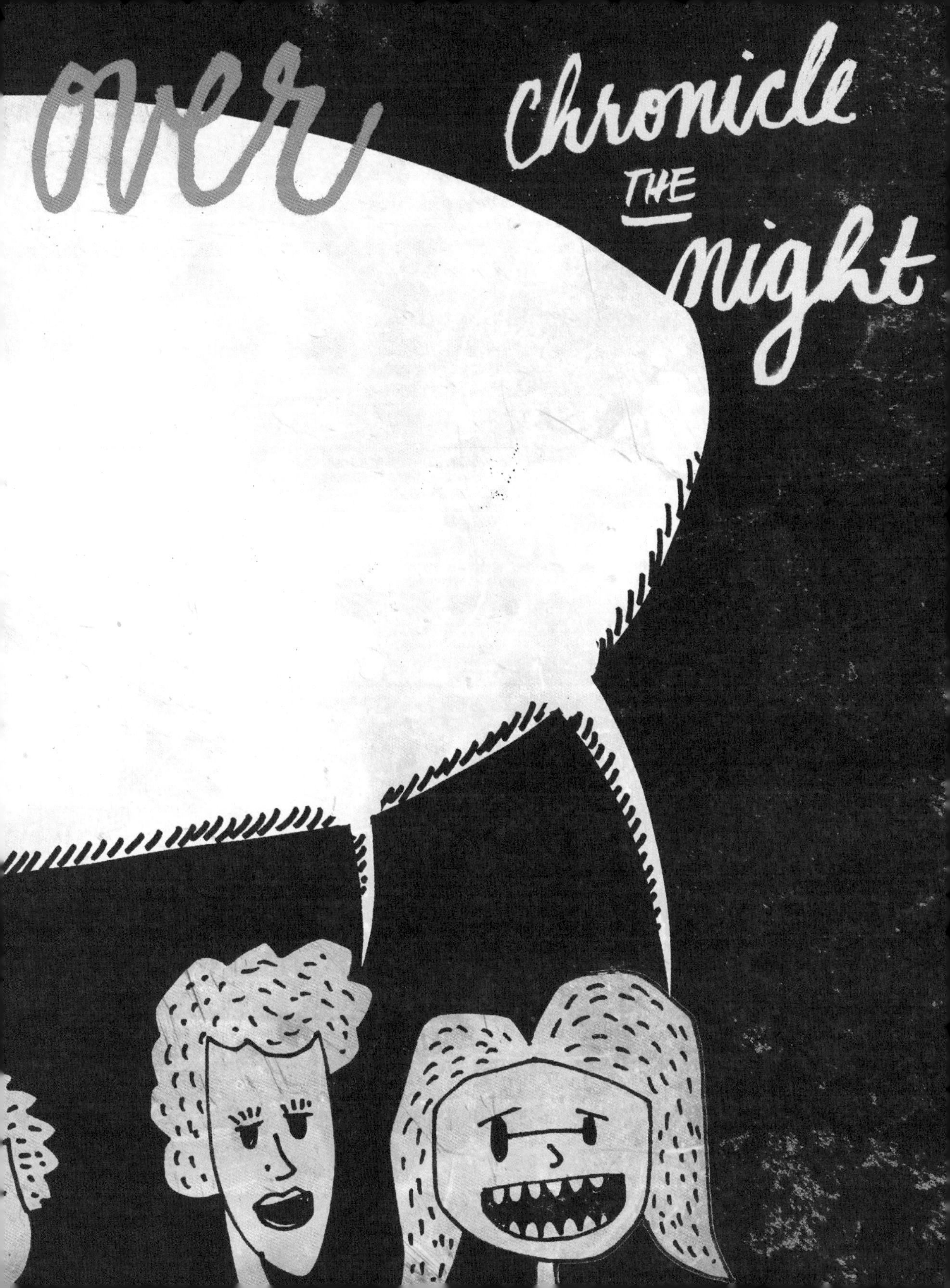

When one of the Bemba people of Zambia stumbles in life, everyone in the village forms a circle around them. Then each member of the tribe recounts every positive thing that person has ever done. The ceremony can last for days.

SHOWER with PRAISE

List ALL the GOOD things you CAN THINK of
ABOUT SOMEONE who NEEDS to KNOW

CREATE TOGETHER

Color together

EAT together

fill THE TABLE with WHAT you SHARED

NELSON MANDELA said that Love COMES MoST Naturally TO THE HUMAN HEART. Don't FIGHT it

IN INDIA and NEPAL, they celebrate HOLI, the festival of LOVE it's hard to HATE THE WORLD WHEN you're HAVING A GIANT color fight THAT Leaves EVERYONE drenched IN fluorescent POWDER

Love
NOTES

WE'RE NOT the FIRST AND WE WON'T BE the Last

NERATIONS

On the Day of the Dead, Mexican families invite the
souls of those who have died to return for a night of celebration.
The festivities start in the cemetery.
From there a path of marigolds lead the dead back home.

CELEBRATE those YOU Lost

WHAT will you ALWAYS REMEMBER?

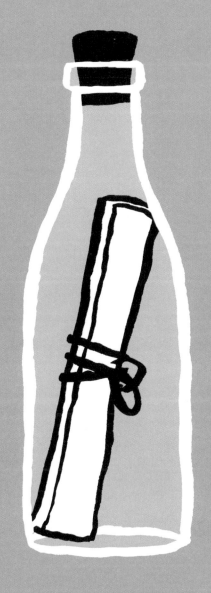

HIDE SOMETHING in your home
FOR FUTURE GENERATIONS to Find

NEVER say GOODBYE

Because good people
have a way of returning to you
at just the right moment.

in SOME tribes of THE FAR NORTH they NEVER SAY GOODBYE BECAUSE they PLAN on COMING BACK

TRACE YOUR HAND

Inside it, write what you'll say
instead of goodbye.

Dream

Believe it

Choose Compassion

Get & Give $5

What do you love doing most? Use it for something bigger.

Go with your PASSION

HERE'S what i'm PASSIONATE about

HERE'S what I DO with IT

When I was little, I really believed in protecting the planet and everyone's place within it. Now, I'm always asking myself: What would my eight-year-old self want? I try to stay true to that.

I was backpacking in Nepal when I first met the incredible women of SASANE. The organization's name means "Let's protect ourselves." Run by female survivors of trafficking, they help some of the thousands of Nepalese women every year who are sold into prostitution or forced labor. By training survivors to be paralegals in police stations, they're making themselves the first point of contact when women who need help come into the legal system.

SASANE took me along on a ten hour journey from Kathmandu, across rickety bridges that tied the mountains together. We arrived at a remote village where the people were warm and open ... but being there was haunting. There were almost no women between the ages of five and fifty.

Friends of friends, someone's cousin, or a distant "well intentioned" acquaintance had come promising good, honest jobs in the city. The villagers thought they were sending their girls off to a better life. They never suspected the truth.

SASANE made a huge impact on the people of that village. It taught them to ask questions and fight for their rights.

Eventually, I had a chance to introduce SASANE to Lee Ann, a corporate lawyer who'd quit her job to travel the world and seek a more meaningful life. Inspired, she came up with a new idea for how to grow the organization. Together, we launched a program where women from SASANE host travelers, teaching them how to make Nepalese dumplings. People from all over the globe, learning from these courageous women, sharing their traditional food: it's hope and community, reborn.

It's easy to feel helpless in the face of all that's wrong in the world, but I say: Speak loudly for what you really believe in. When you have that passion, it's contagious. You'll be amazed by what you can do together.

Adrienne

if it SEEMS
impossible
that's
GOOD

the MOON and the WHALE

There once was a whale
who wanted to journey
all the way to the moon

From balmy waters to icy seas
chasing the beautiful moon

No whale can reach the moon
they say
it's hundreds of thousands of miles
away

But on and on
it made its way
led by the light of the moon

To dive down deep
then rise and leap
O, to touch the moon

Through doldrum days and stormy nights
through rousing songs and painful fights
through sparkling depths and cresting heights
to reach the marvelous moon

Farther and farther on its own track
six thousand miles each season and back
and over time a distance was mapped

As far as the moon
and all the way back

As far as the moon and back!

So this, in the end, is all that we know—
The bigger the dream, the farther you'll go
the greater the distance, the more you will grow

And that's how the journey will change you.

i Dream of...

In 1959, a Tibetan stableman prepared the horses for the Dalai Lama to flee into exile.
Nearly forty years later, the stableman was still living in the barn, waiting for His Holiness to return.
When I met the man, I showed him a picture of the Great Fourteenth, alive and well.
He burst into tears. When you believe in something strongly, people will try to dissuade you.

They'll tell you to stop believing. Don't.

BELIEVE it

THIS is WHAT i BELIEVE

Write your manifesto.

Give

EVERY ACTION HAS A REACTION. WHAT GOES AROUND COMES AROUND. GOODNESS HAS A WAY OF COMING BACK TO YOU.

In China, many people don't believe in saying thank you because it breaks the circle of generosity. They believe in *bao*: acknowledging a gift by giving one back.

禮

what i RECEIVED | what i GAVE BACK

I'll never forget Don Fausto and his mandolin. We met while I was on a work trip to Ometepe Island in Nicaragua. I've never seen such a singer and storyteller. He's the chief of the Los Ramos indigenous people and the eldest person in his community.

Don Fausto uses his music and sense of humor to raise money and materials for his people whenever they're in need. He brings his songs and storytelling from house to house entertaining families, collecting what's required – resources for the local school, food for a family, books for the children. He is a leader who takes care of his people.

His first and most beloved instrument was his mandolin, which had accompanied him for decades, until sadly it was lost. His family sought ways to buy him a new one, but it's complicated when you do not have enough money to support your family's basic needs.

When I learned that Don Fausto's only desire for his 83rd birthday was a mandolin, I was determined to help. As soon as I came back home, I posted his story on my Facebook page. The response was amazing. In less than two days we had collected enough money for a beautiful new mandolin, some extra strings, and some money for his family.

I took the new mandolin with me on my next trip to Nicaragua. It was a magical night. Don Fausto's happiness was indescribable! He told me: "You do not know how thankful I am. This will not be just for me – this beautiful mandolin is something very special that I'm going to pass on to my grandchildren."

I had seen how Don Fausto provided those around him with the things they needed most – joy most of all. I felt so lucky that we were able to do the same for him.

Tania

A Stranger
SHOWED Me this KINDNESS

HERE'S HOW
i passed it on

Choose

Giving is good but caring is better.
Compassion is the key to seeing all
the different ways you can help.

REACH OUT TO Someone
WHO's Living it

We started doing eye clinics in Tanzania, Cambodia and Tibet.
Just think of what it must be like caring for your children when you're blind,
trying to feed and teach and keep them safe. And all it takes is a painless
fifteen minute procedure to change that.

I'll NEVER forget the LOOK on that MOTHER'S face WHEN SHE saw her CHILDREN for the first time IN years

SMALL THINGS i DID that MADE A Difference for SOMEONE ELSE

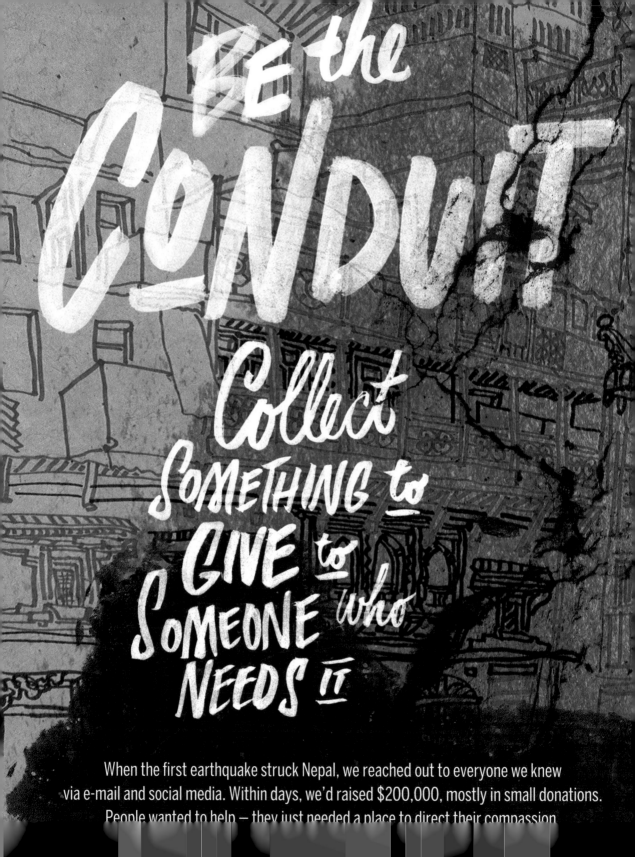

Be the CONDUIT

Collect SOMETHING to GIVE to SOMEONE who NEEDS IT

When the first earthquake struck Nepal, we reached out to everyone we knew via e-mail and social media. Within days, we'd raised $200,000, mostly in small donations. People wanted to help — they just needed a place to direct their compassion.

WHAT did YoU Collect?

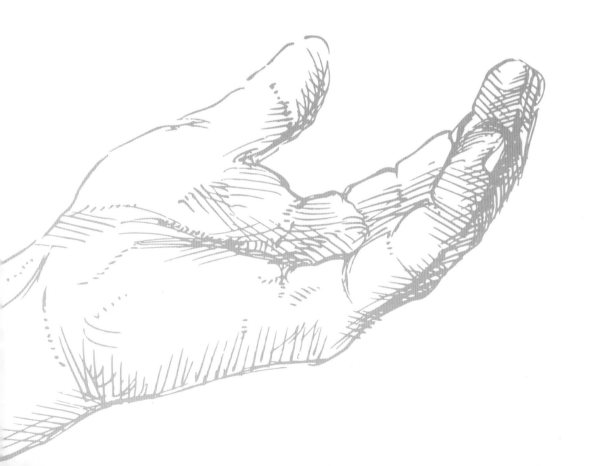

After the typhoon struck the Philippines, I came up with a plan.

In Canada, I gathered giant boxes of used clothing from my musician friends. I scored some incredible stuff!
I had a box of new clothes. I had new designer jeans for teenaged girls. I had shoes. I had baby clothes. We had big sacks of rice and canned goods. The plan wasn't to drop it all off in Manila. I was going to personally take these relief goods off-the-beaten-path.

Our destination was 95 km from civilization. It was a three-and-a-half hour boat ride in a bamboo outrigger held together by twine. The weather was brutal.

We sailed through four meter swells in very rough seas. We kissed the ground when we got there. We were the first boat to land on Tinaga Island in six weeks!

I had planned on taking pictures of the people receiving what I brought. I watched families come into the house where we stayed to get clothes. Families with literally nothing. Nothing at all. Nothing but the t-shirt and shorts they were wearing. No shoes. There is no electricity on this island. There never has been. The kids play with sticks and cans. They might have the nicest beach on the planet, though.

How could I take pictures of them? How could I post pictures of these people online? I put my camera away. I could feel that it would be easier if I wasn't in the house when people came to get stuff.

My friends who donated the goods needed no glory or fame. And I didn't need to be thanked.

gord

GALÁPAGOS

POST

TAKE ONE

LEAVE ONE

In the Galápagos, there is a post office
that travelers know. You will recognize it
by the giant barrel crammed with postcards.

Leave a letter behind and deliver one addressed to someone near you. It can be faster than regular mail.

YOUR
HAPPINESS
COMES
from

CREATING
HAPPINESS
for
OTHERS

THANK you

THIS BOOK TOOK A VILLAGE TO MAKE A REALITY.

It started as an idea to memorialize twenty-five years of building G Adventures, but turned into the mission of a vast group of people who believed that this project could be something truly special and life-changing.

At the top of the list, I have to thank Brad Wilson and the gang at HarperCollins for giving us the freedom to create a book unlike anything that has ever been published, with only a few guidelines along the way. And then my book agent — I know, it sounds weird to me too that I have an agent — Rick Broadhead, who occasionally has the daunting task of having to track me down wherever I am in the world.

The rest I have to thank for their patience and perseverance. The captain of this ship was Josh Greenhut, who looked on what I wanted to create with ever-understanding eyes. He was the wordsmith who guided this project and tamed the massive cast of characters that grew as the project progressed.

I met a group of people in Portland from a company called Mutt Industries, and they really changed my life. Much like when I first went to Tibet in 1997 and experienced people who made decisions based on their spirituality and their hearts, I met a group of outliers at Mutt who showed me a world that is based on creativity and making thoughts beautiful. I have never been so close to people who were determined to create a better visual world and were willing to dedicate their lives to it. Thank you to Steve Luker, Scott Cromer, Cindy Wade, Danny Peterson, Seth Conley, Steven Birch, Neil Kirkpatrick, Eatcho (Mehran Heard), Natsuko Pursell, and the rest of the Mutts. You showed me new levels to which courage can be defined with a pen, pencil or brush.

Next, I'm deeply grateful to the people who contributed their own personal stories to this book: Kavi Guppta, Jasmin Linton, Sokhorn "Con" Yam, Terri Wingham, Vanessa Valenzuela, Kristen Marano, Neil Hamdani, Adrienne Lee, Tania Robles, and Gord Foster. You gave authenticity to the many theories in these pages, and I thank you for being willing to share your stories with the world.

From the G Adventures office, I owe a great deal to Jaymie Bachiu and Andrea Giroux. They were kind of doing their jobs—but I don't remember their job descriptions including countless sleepless nights and having to chase down their boss because he wasn't "feeling it" when it came time to submitting his content to meet "deadlines." I also want to thank Steve English for being the best hugger in the office and always making me sound smart, and Daniel Sendecki for being an affable rogue who can veer from being a bouncer to a gentle poet in the drop of a chapeau.

My name may be on the front of this book, but it's really written by a collective movement that is dedicated to showing people the world in a way that improves wealth distribution and contributes to the greater good. There are so many people who go to war for that idea everyday, and while I can't thank you all here, you know who you are. Thank you for being youer than you.

Bruce

Published by Collins, an imprint of HarperCollins Publishers Ltd.

First edition

HarperCollins books may be purchased for educational, business, or sales promotional use through our Special Markets Department.

HarperCollins Publishers Ltd
2 Bloor Street East, 20th Floor
Toronto, Ontario, Canada, M4W 1A8

www.harpercollins.ca

Library and Archives Canada Cataloguing in Publication information is available upon request.

ISBN 978-1-44344-694-5

Printed and bound in China
PP 10 9 8 7 6 5 4 3 2 1

MAKE

love, art, dinner, notes, friends, mementos, conversation, postcards

#bigsmallthings

hello, Stranger

Love

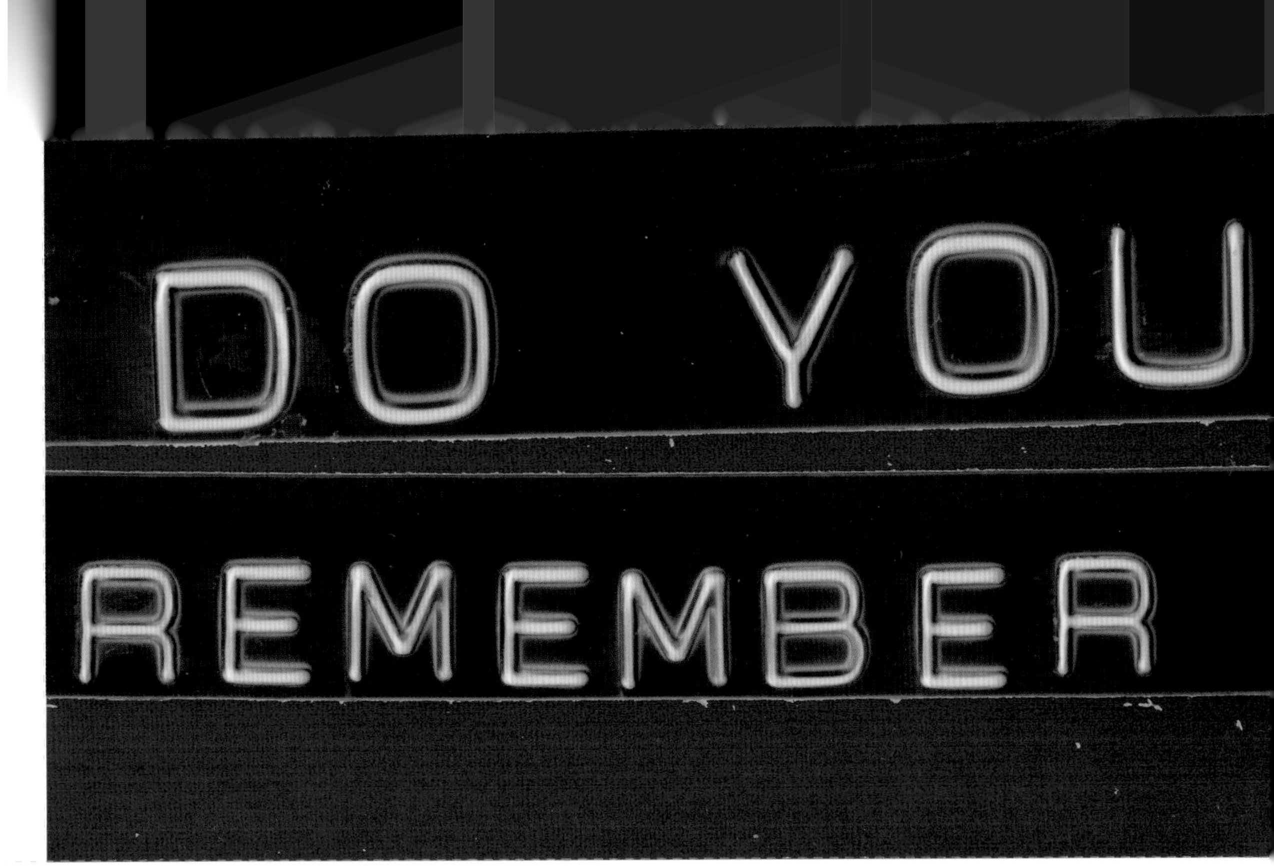
DO YOU
REMEMBER

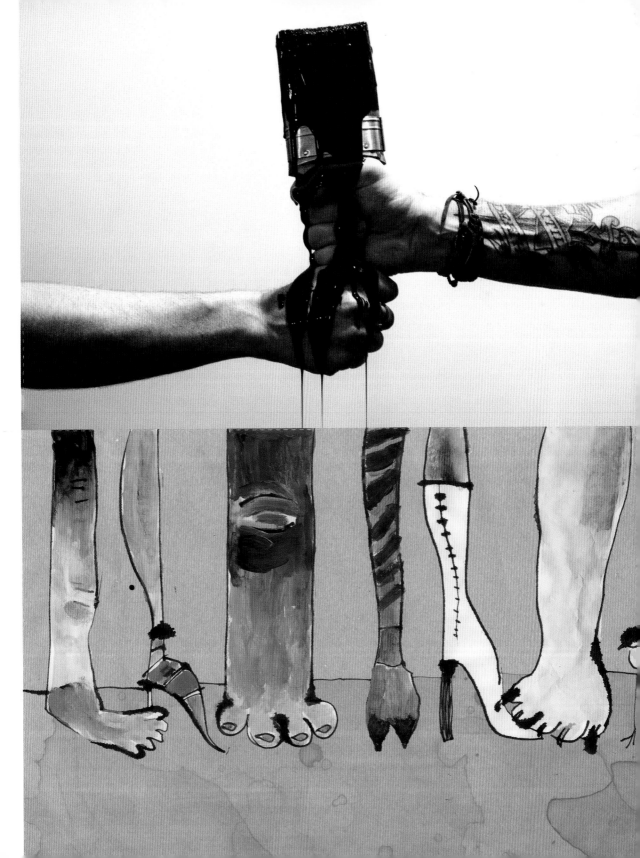

BREATHE
DEEP